11-30-10

Healthy HABITS™

Understanding Cholesterol

Judy Monroe Peterson

rosen central

New York

To Dave, with whom I hope to enjoy life with for a long, long time

Published in 2011 by The Rosen Publishing Group, Inc.
29 East 21st Street, New York, NY 10010

First Edition

Library of Congress Cataloging-in-Publication Data

Peterson, Judy Monroe.
Understanding cholesterol / Judy Monroe Peterson.—1st ed.
    p. cm.—(Healthy habits)
Includes bibliographical references and index.
ISBN 978-1-4358-9440-2 (library binding)
ISBN 978-1-4488-0610-2 (pbk)
ISBN 978-1-4488-0616-4 (6 pack)
1. Cholesterol—Juvenile literature. 2. Coronary heart disease—Prevention—Juvenile literature.
I. Title.
QP752.C5P48 2011
612'.01577—dc22

                                                                    2009052451

Manufactured in Malaysia

CPSIA Compliance Information: Batch #S10YA: For further information, contact Rosen Publishing, New York, New York, at 1-800-237-9932.

CONTENTS

Introduction

Cholesterol is in the news these days. A family member or someone else may take medicine for high cholesterol. Certain foods, such as eggs, are high in cholesterol. Although some foods contain cholesterol, a healthy body makes the cholesterol it needs. The liver in all animals, including humans, makes this soft, waxy substance every day.

Cholesterol is in the blood and in every cell in the body. The body uses cholesterol to form healthy, strong cell membranes (walls). Without cholesterol, cell membranes would be dry and tear easily. Material inside the cells would leak out.

The body uses cholesterol in other ways. Cholesterol is in the tissues of the brain. The non-nerve cells of the brain make cholesterol. The brain is made up of billions of neurons (nerve cells) that communicate with one another. Neurons pass messages to other neurons by releasing chemical substances called neurotransmitters that are located at the ends of neurons. Neurotransmitters cross the gaps between neurons, called synapses, and then bind to nearby neurons. The cholesterol made in the brain helps synapses form.

The body also uses cholesterol to help make certain vitamins and hormones, such as the sex hormones, testosterone and estrogen. Cholesterol is used to make vitamin D, which is necessary for healthy bones and teeth. A small organ called the gallbladder uses cholesterol and other substances to make bile. This green liquid makes it possible for the body to absorb fats. The body uses fats to make fatty tissues that cushion the organs and help keep the body warm.

These teens are competing in a heart healthy recipe contest. By inventing or adapting recipes for the contest, teens can show how delicious healthy food can be.

Cholesterol is essential for children, teens, and adults. Everyone needs it to be healthy. However, some people have high levels of cholesterol. Teens who have high cholesterol are more likely to have high cholesterol as adults. High cholesterol greatly increases the chance of developing cardiovascular disease, which affects the heart and arteries (blood vessels). People who have cardiovascular disease may have a heart attack or stroke, which could result in death. According to the Centers for Disease Control and Prevention (CDC), cardiovascular disease is the main cause of death for adults in the United States.

Children and teens can develop cardiovascular disease. Overweight and obese teens, ages twelve to nineteen, have increased risk. The CDC states that about 20 percent of overweight teens and 43 percent of obese teens have a cholesterol level that raises their chance of cardiovascular heart disease. According to the CDC, about 33 percent of children and teens are overweight or obese. Overweight and obese young people have an increased risk of becoming obese adults and developing high blood pressure, cardiovascular disease, diabetes, and certain cancers.

What teens eat, their fitness levels and weight, and other factors all affect their health. Teens cannot control some factors, such as genetics, that influence their health. However, they can make most of the lifestyle choices that will affect their health now and in the future. Developing and following healthy habits can help teens lead longer, healthier lives.

Chapter 1

Controlling Cholesterol

Cholesterol has many important functions in the body. However, having high levels of cholesterol in the blood is a significant factor for developing cardiovascular disease as teens become older. The higher the cholesterol level, the greater the risk is for developing heart disease or having a heart attack. The National Heart, Lung, and Blood Institute lists heart disease as the number-one cause of death for adults in the United States.

The body makes about 1,000 milligrams of cholesterol every day, mostly in the liver. People might eat another 100 to 500 milligrams every day from certain foods such as meat, egg yolks, and whole milk.

To control cholesterol, a good step is to find out the level of cholesterol in the blood. Teens can do many things to lower their cholesterol if their level is high. If their level is OK, teens can take steps to maintain their healthy level.

Too Much Cholesterol in the Body

Over time, too much cholesterol in the body can damage the circulatory system and many body organs. The circulatory system is made up of the heart, blood, and blood vessels that carry blood

Studies have shown that fatty buildups in arteries, called plaque, begin in childhood and the teen years. To reduce plaque, teens should aim to exercise sixty minutes on most days of the week.

around the body. The heart is the main organ of the circulatory system. About the size of a fist, the heart pumps blood throughout the body.

Blood travels in various directions in the body. Arteries are blood vessels that carry blood filled with oxygen away from the heart. Blood also carries nutrients and other chemicals, such as hormones. Inside the body cells, blood gives up oxygen and picks up waste products. Blood with waste products then flows back to the heart through the veins.

Too much cholesterol in the blood builds up as plaque along the inside walls of the arteries. This buildup is called atherosclerosis, and it is one of the main causes of cardiovascular disease. Atherosclerosis actually begins in childhood and continues as people get older. As atherosclerosis progresses, the arteries become narrow and harden, becoming less flexible. Blood flow through the arteries slows down due to this increased resistance. The heart receives less blood. People may have sharp chest pain if too little blood and oxygen reach the heart. A heart attack can result if the supply of blood to any part of the heart is blocked. If blood supply to the brain is cut off, a stroke can result. Atherosclerosis can also decrease the flow of blood to other organs, such as the kidneys or intestines. This can cause damage to these organs.

High cholesterol can lead to gallstones. These small, hard lumps form in the gallbladder or in the tube that connects the gallbladder to the intestines. Some gallstones are mostly made up of cholesterol. They can block the flow of bile out of the gallbladder, which is a painful condition. A buildup of gallstones can lead to infection or damage of the gallbladder, liver, or pancreas. Death can result if the blockage or infection is not treated.

Transporting Cholesterol Throughout the Body

Cholesterol is a lipid, a type of fat. Blood carries cholesterol throughout the body. However, blood is water-based. Water and fats such as lipids do not mix. To overcome this problem, the body turns cholesterol and other body fats into tiny packages called lipoproteins. Proteins are on the outside of the package, and the fats are on the inside. Lipoproteins readily mix with the blood.

Lipoproteins are made up of three parts: cholesterol, triglycerides, and phospholipids. Triglycerides are a type of fat. They make up most of the fat in the food that people eat. The body needs triglycerides for energy. Phospholipids help lipoproteins stay together.

Main Types of Cholesterol

Two main types of cholesterol are important in the health of the body: low-density lipoprotein (LDL) and high-density lipoprotein (HDL). Both types travel in the blood.

People often call LDL the "bad cholesterol." LDL carries more than half of the total blood cholesterol in the blood to tissues. Some LDL is returned to the liver. LDL is the most common lipoprotein in the body. However, too much LDL in the blood can cause atherosclerosis in the arteries that bring blood to the heart and brain. This increases the risk of heart attack and stroke.

HDL is known as the "good cholesterol." It acts in opposite ways from LDL by picking up extra cholesterol out of cells and tissues, including from plaque in the blood vessels, and bringing it to the liver. The liver reuses the cholesterol or makes bile from it. By keeping plaque from building up, HDL helps protect against cardiovascular disease. HDL may provide another benefit. It is made up of certain

THE CORONARY ARTERIES

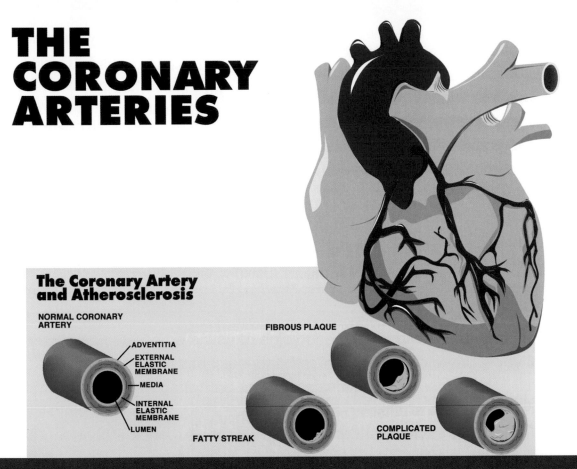

The Coronary Artery and Atherosclerosis

NORMAL CORONARY ARTERY

FIBROUS PLAQUE

ADVENTITIA

EXTERNAL ELASTIC MEMBRANE

MEDIA

INTERNAL ELASTIC MEMBRANE

LUMEN

FATTY STREAK

COMPLICATED PLAQUE

The buildup of plaque in coronary arteries occurs in three stages. It begins as a yellow, fatty streak in muscle cells. Over time, fibrous plaque develops that projects into arteries. Then blood clots can form, leading to complicated plaque.

molecules that may prevent LDL from being changed into a lipoprotein likely to cause cardiovascular disease.

Risk Factors for Developing High Cholesterol

A number of risk factors can contribute to developing high cholesterol. Teens cannot control some of these risk factors, such as

Triglycerides and Cardiovascular Disease

Triglycerides are the most common type of fat in the body. They provide much of the energy needed for cells to function. The body turns extra food eaten into triglycerides and stores them in fat cells. When needed, the body changes triglycerides into energy that the body uses. Normal triglyceride levels vary by age and gender (male or female). Like high levels of cholesterol, too many triglycerides in the blood can increase the risk of cardiovascular disease. People who have high levels of triglycerides often have high levels of LDL. They also tend to have low levels of HDL. High levels of triglycerides combined with high levels of LDL tend to speed up the process of atherosclerosis, increasing the risk for heart attack and stroke. Many people with heart disease, diabetes, or both have high triglyceride levels.

heredity, ethnicity, gender, and age. A teen's genes influence LDL cholesterol by affecting how fast LDL is made and removed from the blood. A tendency toward high cholesterol runs in some families. A parent, brother, or sister with high cholesterol or cardiovascular disease increases the chance of a teen having high cholesterol. If a teen has high cholesterol and a parent or sibling has cardiovascular disease before the age of fifty-five, the teen has a greater risk of developing cardiovascular disease. Male and female African American teens have slightly lower cholesterol levels than other ethnic groups, including Caucasians and Mexican Americans.

The cholesterol level of children slowly increases from age two to ten. After that, cholesterol levels for teens tend to rise according to

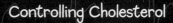

The students in this photo are handing out strawberries during lunch. They are promoting a different fruit or vegetable every month to encourage teens to choose healthy foods.

gender. Until the age of fifty, males are more likely to have high blood cholesterol than females. After fifty, a slightly higher percent of females than males have high cholesterol.

Teens can control a major risk factor: behavior. Making healthful choices in the teen years can help reduce the risk of developing high cholesterol and cardiovascular disease later in life. Some of the behavioral risk factors that teens can control include diet, exercise, weight, smoking, and stress. By controlling behavioral risk factors, teens are better able to reduce the risks of developing high blood pressure, diabetes, and high cholesterol.

Checking Cholesterol Levels

The American Academy of Pediatrics (AAP) recommends a cholesterol test for teens who are obese. The AAP also recommends testing if the family history for high cholesterol is unknown, but a child has risk factors for high cholesterol, such as obesity, diabetes, or high blood pressure. Teens should have their cholesterol levels checked if they have these same risk factors.

Cholesterol testing is not usually done for children or teens under the age of twenty. To get cholesterol levels checked, teens first need to see their doctor. At the appointment, the doctor will ask about medical history, family history of high cholesterol or heart disease, allergies, medications, and health habits. The doctor will probably conduct a physical exam. If teens have one or more risk factors for high cholesterol, the doctor will request a blood test called a lipid panel or lipid profile to check cholesterol levels.

To get accurate test results, people must fast twelve hours before their blood draw. They cannot eat or drink anything but water before the test. Because of this, teens may want to ask that their blood be drawn early in the morning. After the blood draw, they can eat and go to school or go home.

The doctor will typically need a week or more to analyze the lipid panel and other information. Then the doctor will talk with teens about their results by telephone or by an appointment to speak in person. When teens get their results, they will see a set of four numbers. The numbers are total cholesterol, LDL cholesterol, HDL cholesterol, and triglycerides. In the United States, cholesterol levels are measured in milligrams (mg) of cholesterol per deciliter (dL) of blood. According to the American Heart Association, the

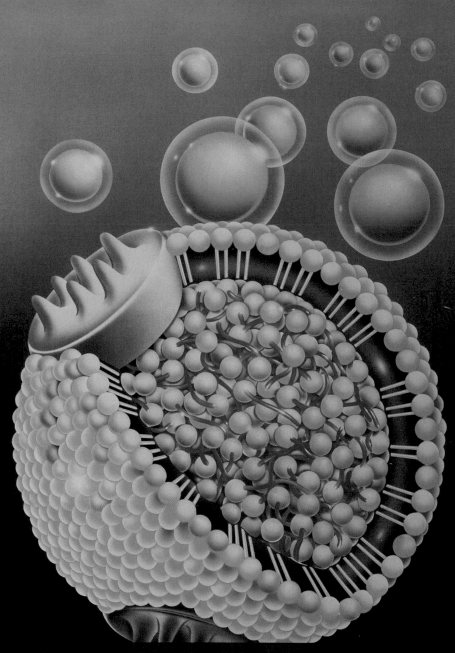

The low-density lipoprotein (LDL) particle is a type of cholesterol in the blood. Proteins (pink), phospholipids (green), and cholesterol (yellow) are found in the outer coat. Cholesterol is also within the core of LDL particles.

following are cholesterol levels in healthy children and teens from two to nineteen years old:

	Total Cholesterol (mg/dL)	LDL Cholesterol (mg/dL)	HDL Cholesterol (mg/dL)	Triglycerides (mg/dL)
Desirable	Less than 170	Less than 110		
Borderline	170–199	110–129		
High	200 or greater	130 or greater		
Should be			Greater than or equal to 35	Less than or equal to 150

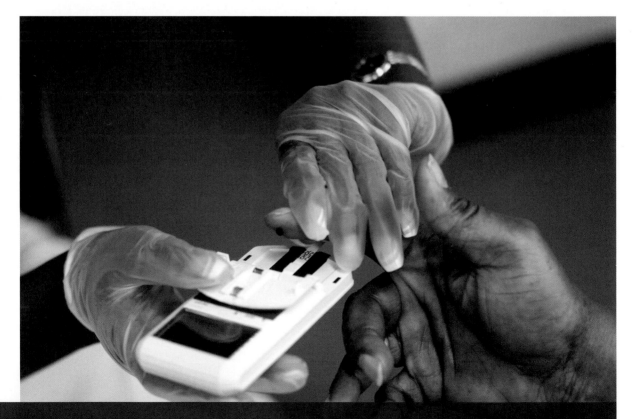

A nurse is taking a blood sample to find out a man's cholesterol level at a health fair in Newark, New Jersey.

If at risk for heart disease, a teen's target levels may be different. Sometimes a first test shows normal cholesterol levels for teens at risk. The doctor might want to have them take another cholesterol test. If the results are still OK, teens should take the fasting cholesterol test again in three to five years.

The American Heart Association reports that about 9.6 percent of those between the ages of twelve to nineteen have total cholesterol levels higher than 200 mg/dL. However, many teens and adults don't know that they have high blood cholesterol because the condition usually does not have symptoms.

If teens have risk factors for high cholesterol, it is important for them to find out their cholesterol numbers. Lowering high cholesterol levels lessens the risk for developing cardiovascular disease, which reduces the chance of a heart attack or stroke now and as they age. Teens can take many steps to reduce high cholesterol levels or maintain healthy ones, including healthy eating, exercise, and more.

Chapter 2

Changing What You Eat

One way that teens can affect their cholesterol levels is by the foods they eat. The body makes all the cholesterol it needs. Teens do not need to eat additional cholesterol to be healthy. However, some fat in the diet is necessary. Fats are an important source of energy for the body, and they carry vitamins A, D, E, and K into the blood. They are also a source of linoleic acid, an essential fatty acid that the body cannot make. Linoleic acid is required for healthy skin and growth. Eating a diet that is low in cholesterol and certain fats can help lower cholesterol levels in the blood and maintain healthy levels.

Fats That Can Affect Cholesterol Levels

Three types of dietary fats can increase blood cholesterol levels: cholesterol, saturated fats, and trans fats. Cholesterol is found only in animal products, including red meat, poultry (chicken and turkey), shellfish, egg yolks, and whole-milk dairy foods like butter, cheese, cream, and ice cream. Reduced-fat dairy foods, such as 2 percent or 1 percent milk or yogurt, have some cholesterol. Plant-based foods—vegetables, fruit, and whole grains—generally do not contain cholesterol.

Saturated fats are solid or semisolid at room temperature. They are found naturally in many foods, such as red meat, poultry with skin,

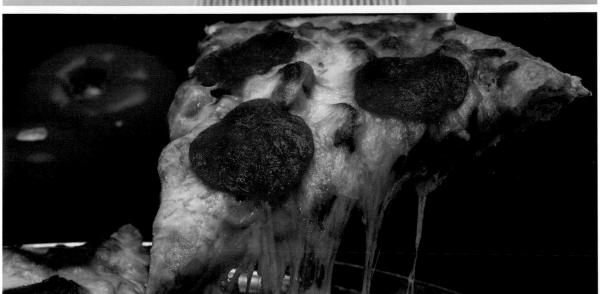

Ice cream and pizza typically contain lots of cholesterol and saturated fats. These fats, along with trans fats found in pizza crust and other baked or fried foods, can contribute to increased blood cholesterol levels. Eat these foods only occasionally.

whole-milk foods, lard (pork fat), and tropical oils. Tropical oils include coconut oil, cocoa butter, palm oil, and palm kernel oil. Most saturated fat that people eat comes from animal and dairy foods. Saturated fats can increase both cholesterol and triglyceride levels in the blood.

Most trans fats are found in foods that are baked or fried in factories, restaurants, bakeries, fast-food places, and cafeterias. To

Olive oil is one type of plant oil that is high in unsaturated fats. Studies have shown that these fats may lower total blood cholesterol levels when eaten in small amounts.

make trans fats, food companies use a process called hydrogenation. They add hydrogen to liquid vegetable oils to change them into solid fats. Foods that contain trans fats can last a long time. Shortening and margarine are trans fats. Fried or baked foods on grocery store shelves that often contain trans fats are potato chips, bread, crackers, cookies, muffins, doughnuts, pies, piecrust, and cakes.

Unsaturated fats may actually lower total blood cholesterol levels when used to replace saturated fats and trans fats. Plant oils are typically liquid at room temperature. They are usually high in unsaturated fats. Plant oils include olive oil, canola oil, vegetable oil, peanut oil, flaxseed oil, corn oil, soybean oil, and safflower oil. Other plants oils are used for flavoring, such as walnut oil and

Eating grilled salmon is one way to reduce fat in the diet. Also avoid deep-fried foods, and choose white poultry meat instead of dark, which has more fat.

sesame oil. Nuts, avocados, olives, and some fish are naturally high in unsaturated fats.

Reducing Cholesterol and Fat

Teens who reduce cholesterol, saturated fats, and trans fats in their diets are taking important steps toward lowering their blood cholesterol and triglyceride levels. A healthy diet includes some fat. However, most people need only a limited amount. The Dietary Guidelines for Americans recommends that teens have a total daily fat intake of 25 to 35 percent of calories. The total daily fat depends on the gender, age, and activity level of each teen. The Department of Health and Human Services and the U.S. Department of Agriculture update the Dietary Guidelines every five years.

Teens can think of ways to cut back on the types and amounts of fat they eat. A good starting point is to focus on cholesterol, saturated fats, and trans fats. Limit foods that are high in cholesterol, such as egg yolks, organ meats like liver, and foods that contain whole milk. Cholesterol-free egg substitutes or egg whites can replace egg yolks. Egg whites do not have cholesterol. To reduce fat, eat beef, pork, or lamb labeled "loin" or "sirloin."

Go with selections that are fat-free, 1 percent fat, and low-fat when consuming milk-based foods. Tub margarines with liquid vegetable oil listed as the first ingredient are also good choices, but use only a little at meals. Sometimes butter and cream are in casseroles, sauces, and desserts. It is OK to eat butter, cream, and ice cream in small amounts for special occasions. These dairy foods have more cholesterol and saturated fat than whole milk. When preparing and eating food, replace butter with olive oil and other heart-healthy plant oils.

A healthy diet that includes plenty of vegetables and fruits is a great way to fight cardiovascular disease. These plant foods are typically low in fats and do not contain cholesterol.

Teens can choose lean meats, poultry, fish, and seafood cooked without saturated and trans fats. Grilling, baking, boiling, steaming, and broiling are healthy ways to cook food. Shrimp has more cholesterol than other types of fish and seafood. However, shrimp is lower in saturated fat and total fat than most meats and poultry.

Another way to reduce cholesterol and fats is to eat fewer packaged foods. Many snacks and desserts are made with saturated fats and trans fats. French fries, onion rings, doughnuts, and other foods are sometimes fried in trans fats. Processed meats, such as sausages, hot dogs, and salami, are high in saturated fats. Eating less high-fat salad dressing and mayonnaise are small, but important, steps as well.

Choosing a Healthy Diet

Vegetables, fruits, and whole-grain foods get special attention in a healthy diet. Eating plenty of these foods every day can help teens follow a diet that is low in cholesterol and saturated and trans fats. These foods also contribute to daily fiber. Although fiber cannot be digested and used as energy by the body, it can help lower blood cholesterol. Foods high in fiber tend to be lower in fat and calories. Fiber makes a person feel full, so he or she won't eat as much. The Dietary Guidelines recommends that teens eat 25 grams of fiber every day. To avoid constipation from a diet high in fiber, people should drink six to eight glasses of water every day.

Teens can replace high-fat foods with fruits and vegetables. These plant foods are low in fats and calories and provide important fiber, vitamins, and minerals. A healthy goal is 2 ½ to 3 cups (575 to 690 grams) of vegetables and 1 ½ to 2 cups (345 to 460 grams) of fruit every day. Teens can think of eating the colors of the rainbow: red, orange, yellow, white, green, blue, and purple. Some colorful vegetables and fruits include spinach, kale, broccoli, carrots, peaches, oranges, kiwi, and berries.

Whole grains are another important part of a healthy diet. There are many choices: whole wheat, oatmeal, whole rye, whole barley, and whole corn. Other whole grains are bulgur (cracked wheat), pop-corn, brown rice, wild rice, quinoa, millet, buckwheat, and triticale. Whole grains should be the first ingredient on the food label of store-bought breads, crackers, and other baked foods. It is recommended

To determine the amount of fats in foods, teens can read the food package label. It tells how many grams of fat and what kinds of fats are in each serving.

that a person eat bread with at least 3 grams of dietary fiber per slice, whole-grain pastas, and brown rice.

Teens can choose healthier, unsaturated fats like olive oil and nut oils. Limiting fats and oil that are high in saturated and trans fats is another good step to take. Eat good fats sparingly, such as ¼ cup (114 grams) of nuts, one tablespoon of seeds (like sunflower seeds) or peanut butter, five olives, or one slice of avocado daily. Poultry, dry beans and peas, and dairy choices should be lean, low-fat, or fat-free. Eating fish two or more times each week is also important in a healthy diet.

Lowering Cholesterol with Omega-3 Fatty Acids

A healthy eating plan should include an unsaturated fat called omega-3 fatty acid. This fat can help reduce triglyceride levels and lower blood pressure. Fatty, cold-water fish such as herring, tuna, salmon, trout, and mackerel contain high levels of omega-3 fatty acids. The American Heart Association recommends eating two 3-ounce (85 grams) servings of cold-water fish once every week. Teens who can't eat fish or don't like it can take a fish oil or algal oil supplement that provides omega-3 fatty acids, but they should be careful not to take too much. A doctor or dietician can recommend how much fish oil or algal oil supplement to take. Canola oil, flaxseed oil, soybean oil, and walnuts are also good sources of omega-3 fatty acids. Some packaged foods and beverages contain added omega-3 fatty acids, such as milk-based foods, juices, salad dressings, breakfast cereals, and bread.

Changing Eating Habits

When it comes to eating, everyone has his or her habits. Some are good, such as eating whole-grain cereals with skim milk and fruit for breakfast. Others are not as good, such as regularly having high-fat snacks in the afternoons or before bed. Teens may need to change some of their eating habits. Some changes can be fairly easy—for instance, adding more vegetables and fruits to the diet by consuming vegetable-based casseroles, steamed vegetables, and low-fat soups. Seasonal fruits make great snacks instead of high-fat chips or candy. Desserts like candy, cakes, muffins, pies, cookies, and ice cream often contain a lot of fat. If choosing these sweet treats, eat a small amount at the end of a healthy meal only occasionally.

Some schools are fighting obesity by having vending machines that stock healthy foods. This way, teens can't buy foods with little nutritional value such as candy, chips, and soft drinks in school.

Changing eating habits may take a little thought, time, and practice. One good habit is to read food labels and the list of ingredients. Both provide a lot of useful information. Use food labels to learn portion size and the types and amount of fats in a serving. For instance, a ½ cup (114 grams) serving of low-fat ice cream or other treat should have no more than 3 grams of saturated fat. The terms "hydrogenated," "partially hydrogenated," "shortening," and "interesterified" on a food label means the product contains trans fats.

Healthy eating requires consuming a variety of foods. Teens might need to plan meals and snacks to eat less fast food. These foods are often high in fat, salt, and sugar. Eating at fast-food restaurants is OK every once in a while, but not every day. Here are some tips when eating out: Don't super-size a meal. Choose a simple hamburger, leaving off the sauce, cheese, and bacon. Eat a baked potato with a small serving of sour cream, or have a small serving of fries occasionally. Salads are fine, but use low-calorie dressing and go easy on the cheese, fatty meats, crispy chicken, noodles, and croutons. Watch for trans fats. Most biscuits, pizza dough, piecrust, and other pastries contain trans fats. Many fast-food restaurants use trans fat oils over and over in deep-fry cookers.

Teens might keep a food diary for a few days to help them learn about their food patterns. In the diary, they write everything they eat and when they eat it. Afterward they look for patterns, such as eating high-fat sweets after every supper. They can then replace unhealthy habits with new, healthy ones. For example, they can decide to eat more slowly so that they are less likely to overeat. Instead of eating when stressed or tired, teens can plan alternatives like taking a walk or talking to a friend. Teens may need to pay attention to when they are truly hungry and not eat when they are tired, anxious, or bored.

Spread food out over the course of a day by eating breakfast, lunch, dinner, and a healthy snack. This provides the body with a steady supply of energy. Avoid vending machines by planning ahead and stashing some snacks with fiber. An apple, orange, or a handful of almonds or whole-grain crackers are all healthy snacks.

A doctor or dietician can provide meal plans and tips for maintaining a low-cholesterol diet. Cookbooks on low-fat cooking, which can be found at local libraries, and Web sites also give many ideas for reducing cholesterol and saturated fats and having a healthy diet. The amount of food to eat each day varies with a teen's age, gender, height, weight, and activity level. The Web site MyPyramid. gov offers free eating plans and interactive tools to help teens make well-balanced food choices and track their meals based on the Dietary Guidelines.

Small and large changes to eating habits can help teens lower their cholesterol and triglyceride levels. What teens eat is as important as their physical activity. Like healthy eating, regular exercise may help lower total blood cholesterol levels.

MYTHS and FACTS

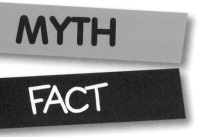
MYTH People need to eat cholesterol to stay healthy.

FACT The body makes all the cholesterol it needs. People do not need to eat foods that have cholesterol to be healthy.

MYTH People should not eat eggs because they have a lot of cholesterol.

FACT One egg has about two-thirds the recommended daily amount of cholesterol, which is contained in the yolk. However, eggs are an excellent source of protein. People can eat an egg or two on a given day, but they should limit other sources of cholesterol for that day if they eat the yolks.

MYTH Cholesterol levels can be reduced by eating soy-based foods, such as soy nuts, tofu, soymilk, and soy burgers.

FACT Soy has no effect on HDL "good" cholesterol and only minimally reduces LDL "bad" cholesterol.

Chapter 3

Exercise Can Help

Regular exercise can reduce low-density lipoprotein (LDL) cholesterol (bad cholesterol) and triglycerides. At the same time, exercise increases high-density lipoprotein (HDL) cholesterol (good cholesterol). The result is better blood flow because the buildup of plaque in the arteries is lowered. In turn, the risk of cardiovascular disease, stroke, and heart attack is lowered.

More Benefits of Exercise

Exercise provides many major benefits. It strengthens the muscles, skeleton, and other moving parts of the body. It helps make the heart stronger and work more efficiently. The heart is a muscle and needs regular exercise just like muscles in the arms and legs. Exercise improves the circulatory system by temporarily expanding arteries and strengthening them. More blood circulates, thereby decreasing blood pressure.

Exercise helps the lungs work better. When exercising, people breathe from the diaphragm (a strong, thin muscle below the lungs). When breathing in, the diaphragm and muscles around the lungs contract. Air rushes into the lungs. Air fills the lungs and brain and body tissues. The rib cage expands, and lung volume increases.

Teens generally do better in school when they get regular exercise. Brain waves responsible for quick thinking fire faster. Concentration is also improved.

When breathing out, the diaphragm and other muscles relax. Breathing from the diaphragm is called deep breathing. Teens who exercise regularly increase their lung capacity. This means they don't feel out of breath while walking up four flights of stairs or running to catch a ball.

Other benefits of exercise include better sleep, body toning, and improved posture and coordination. Teens who are fit respond quickly to stimuli, which helps when they drive, cycle, or play sports. Many teens find that exercising relieves stress and anxiety, improves mood, and enhances self-esteem. A strong body can restore itself faster after being sick. Getting regular exercise helps improve concentration, which can help teens do better in school.

Regular physical activity can increase the HDL, or "good" cholesterol in the blood. Stretching is also part of being physically fit. It increases flexibility and reduces the risk of injuries.

Exercising can help teens lose weight and maintain a healthy body weight. It speeds up metabolism (the process by which the body gets energy from food). This can help keep teens from developing high cholesterol or diabetes, or becoming overweight or obese. Physically healthy teens have higher energy levels for longer periods of time. Exercise is fun, too!

Five Fitness Areas for Health

Teens need regular exercise to keep healthy. The more muscles and joints that are worked, the greater the gain in physical and mental health. Develop a fitness routine that covers the following five areas: aerobic fitness, muscular fitness, stretching, core exercise, and balance training.

Aerobic Fitness

Most exercise programs include aerobic exercise, also called cardio or endurance activity. Aerobic exercise is any physical activity that uses large muscle groups and increases the heart rate for a period of time. During aerobics, breathing becomes faster and deeper. The heart pumps more oxygen to the muscles to be used to do more work. When teens are aerobically fit, their heart, lung, and blood vessels transport oxygen through their body more efficiently. They have more energy to do activities.

According to the American Academy of Pediatrics, teens should get sixty minutes or more of aerobic activity every day. Examples include walking briskly, jogging, hiking, skiing, biking, water aerobics, dancing, and swimming laps. Other water fitness exercises are water polo, kayaking, canoeing, and rowing. Daily activities like washing the car, raking leaves, vacuuming, and shoveling snow from a driveway are also aerobic exercise. Some teens play sports. Basketball, soccer, football, and competitive swimming are all examples of aerobic sports.

Before an aerobic workout, the body needs a warm-up to avoid muscle strain or injury. Warming up prepares the body for aerobic activity. It slowly boosts the heart rate and body temperature, and it increases blood flow to the muscles. To warm up, choose an activity that works the same muscles that will be used during the aerobic exercise. Before a long run, for example, jog, walk, or march slowly for five to ten minutes, and then gradually increase the pace. Right after a workout, cool down for five to ten minutes. Teens can do the same activities to warm up and cool down.

Muscular Fitness

Muscular fitness through strength training is another important part of a fitness program. The more work muscles do, the stronger they become. Strength training two or three times every week is recommended. It helps increase both muscle fitness and bone strength. Schools and fitness centers offer many resistance machines, free weights, and other tools to work out with. Teens can work out at home with hand and ankle weights. In place of machines, teens can use resistance bands or canned food as weights, or they can make weights by filling containers with water or sand. No tools are needed when the body's own weight is used to do exercises like push-ups, pull-ups, crunches, planks, and squats.

Stretching

Stretching muscles regularly is important because aerobic and strength-training exercises contract (shorten) the muscles. Stretching improves flexibility and posture, and it's a good stress reliever. A great time to do stretching is after exercising because the muscles are warm and better able to stretch. Some teens prefer to stretch before and after exercising. Practicing yoga is also a good way to stretch.

Core Exercise

The core muscles are the muscles of the trunk: stomach, lower back, hips, and pelvis. These muscles serve as the center of energy for movements like bending over to put on shoes and lifting textbooks to the top shelf in a locker. Core exercises, such as crunches and

A fitness program helps lower cholesterol levels. To stick with an exercise program, teens can take classes, use a wellness coach, or find something that motivates them such as maintaining a healthy weight.

squats, use the trunk of the body without support. Improving core strength results in better posture, strong stomach muscles, and reduced muscle injury. Core exercises strengthen the muscles that support the spine, which improves coordination between the upper and lower body. Some teens like to do core exercises on a stability or balance ball. Aim for three or more times each week of doing core-strengthening exercises.

Balance Training

Balance training can help improve and maintain balance. The brain, bones, and muscles work together to keep the body balanced. Good

Finding Time for Physical Fitness

Finding time to exercise can be challenging for teens. They usually have a full schedule that includes school, schoolwork, lessons, after-school jobs, clubs, and time with friends and family. One way to free up time is to keep screen time to two hours or less a day. Screen time includes time watching television, playing video or computer games, and using the computer. Another way is to make exercising part of a daily routine. Just as they do with other important activities, teens should plan and schedule workouts and exercise classes. It's OK to take a little time off from exercising. People should listen to their bodies and not force a workout or exercise session when feeling too tired or ill. They might want to take a day or two off and then return to their regular fitness routine when feeling better.

• • •

balance helps keep the body stable, which reduces falls and injuries. Balance exercises that are done two or three times each week help strengthen the stabilizing muscles in knees, ankles, and hips. Activities like tai chi can promote balance. A simple balance exercise is to stand up and sit down without using the hands. Another is to close the eyes and stand on one leg for fifteen to thirty seconds, then switch to the other leg. Work up to a few minutes on each leg.

Where to Work Out

Teens can train at home, outside, in fitness centers, at school, or other places. Strength-training exercises, such as push-ups or crunches, or aerobic exercises like jumping rope, walking, or running may be simple to fit in during the day. Swimming laps is another type of cardiovascular exercise. Some teens may already know how to swim, while others might want to take lessons. Recreation centers, YMCAs, swim schools, and community education programs hold swimming and other fitness classes.

Before working out for the first time at a fitness center, teens should set up an appointment with a trainer at the center. The trainer will explain how to use the equipment and how best to train by doing the correct number of repetitions and using the right amount of weight. Many teens enjoy taking group classes such as teen hip-hop and teen kickboxing. Some fitness centers change the schedule of classes and instructors to keep people interested and motivated.

Sticking with a Fitness Plan

Sometimes people start fitness programs, but stop because they get bored or the results are not obvious right away. To stay motivated, teens can set short-term, medium-term, and long-term training goals. The goals must be realistic so that they can be achieved. Examples are the following: a short-term goal of walking fifteen minutes each day, medium-term goal of walking thirty minutes four or five times every week, and a long-term goal of competing in a 5K (3 mile) walk or run. Some teens like to write down their goals and track their progress. Anyone who has not been exercising should start slowly with a basic program, gradually adding more challenging exercises. Pushing too hard at first might cause pain or injuries.

Keeping fitness exercises interesting helps people stick with their fitness plans. Some teens cross-train. Cross-training combines two or more types of physical activity. For instance, teens might alternate biking with swimming laps or jogging. They could play a team sport

Reps

Cardio Exercise
jogging

Time/Distance
1 mile

Teens can set short-term and long-term goals for regular exercise. To track their progress, they can keep an activity log that includes the activity, workout date and time, and how long they did the activity.

like soccer and take an aerobics class on alternate days. In addition to adding interest, cross-training gives the bones, muscles, and joints a rest from repeated movements. It can also help reduce the risk of injuries.

Adding variety to a fitness plan could come from trying something new, such as joining a health club, martial arts center, hiking group, or softball league. For a change, some teens do their stretching, core exercises, and balance exercises outside. Other ways to keep a fitness routine going are to use different machines, change the length of exercise sessions, and change how often specific exercises or routines are done. Teens who are involved in sports might want to do sport-specific training that focuses on technique and safety.

Sixty minutes of aerobic exercise every day may be easier to achieve than teens realize. For instance, climbing stairs, taking the dog for a run, and cutting the lawn are aerobic exercises that add up during a day. Washing windows and running the vacuum cleaner through the house for fifteen minutes are other examples. Ten minutes of exercising four to six times per day can provide some cholesterol-lowering benefits. For example, teens can use hand weights or resistance tubing or bands while listening to music or talking on the phone.

Exercise can be more fun if a person does it with a friend. Teens might want to find an exercise buddy or join a sports team at school or at a community center. By taking classes at a local fitness center or YMCA, teens may meet new people and make new friends. Being fit is for life, and the ways to keep fit are endless. Teens who find something they like and make daily physical activity fun are likely to make it a habit that they will keep. In addition to keeping fit, teens have many other ways to help improve or maintain their cholesterol levels.

Ten Great Questions

1 What is the recommended amount of cholesterol per day?

2 Does red meat have more cholesterol than chicken or turkey?

3 Is it a good idea to eat packaged foods with added sterols or stanols, substances that help block the absorption of cholesterol?

4 Can eating more dietary fiber lower blood cholesterol?

5 Are home cholesterol test kits accurate?

6 Is cholesterol the only thing that causes the buildup of plaque in the arteries?

7 Can having very low cholesterol levels cause health problems?

8 Can some medications affect cholesterol levels?

9 What is a good weight-loss exercise plan that will help lower total cholesterol levels?

10 Can secondhand smoke increase total cholesterol levels?

Chapter 4

Other Healthy Habits for Lowering Cholesterol

Lifestyle changes are key to improving cholesterol levels. Focusing on healthy habits such as increasing physical activity, eating well, and losing extra weight can bring the numbers down. Other ways to improve cholesterol levels include practicing stress management and getting enough sleep. HDL cholesterol improves when people quit smoking. The goal of lifestyle changes is to develop healthy habits that help lower total cholesterol levels.

Losing Weight

Being overweight or obese can contribute to high levels of total blood cholesterol. Losing weight depends on how many calories a teen eats and burns. If fewer calories are eaten than burned, a teen will lose weight. Even losing 10 percent of extra weight can help lower total cholesterol levels.

To lose weight, it's a good idea to make a plan that includes both a healthy diet and daily physical activity. To start, teens need to figure out how much weight to lose safely. Health professionals use the body mass index (BMI) to calculate a person's body fat. A BMI number is the ratio of weight to height. To calculate their BMIs, teens can

By combining a heart-healthy diet with regular exercise, teens can lose weight and keep it off. Losing weight can lower the risk of developing cardiovascular diseases.

enter their height and weight into a calculator on the Centers for Disease Control and Prevention Web site at http://apps.nccd.cdc. gov/dnpabmi. A BMI between 18 and 25 is considered healthy.

The next step is choosing a target weight within a healthy range. Teens can use their current BMI to determine a target BMI and its corresponding healthy weight. A doctor or dietician can also provide information on target BMIs and weights. Once teens know their starting weight and target weight, they can set safe, realistic goals for weight loss and make a plan. Losing ½ to 1 pound (0.2 to 0.5 kg) each week is a healthy goal. Losing too much weight too quickly can

Fad diets can be unhealthy because they deprive the body of important nutrients. Teens risk damaging their bones and organs, and even brain tissue. Constantly losing and gaining weight stresses the heart, lungs, and immune system.

have dire consequences. Teens might want to write their plan down, including their goals. Some teens keep a diary or journal to help them stick to their plan.

Diet and exercise are equal partners when it comes to losing weight. The best way to lose weight is by eating fewer calories and burning more calories with regular exercise. This strategy works no matter how much weight a teen wants to lose. Another strategy is eating more whole grains, vegetables, and fruit and less of foods high in fat and sugar. It's OK to eat favorite foods that are high in calories, but only enjoy a small amount occasionally. Avoid fad diets as a way to lose weight. Fad diets promise quick ways to drop extra pounds. Some fad diets claim a large or quick weight loss of more than 1 to 2 pounds (0.5 to 0.9 kg) per week. Others promote special foods, such as grapefruit or cabbage soup, that claim to help in taking off weight. Still others eliminate a food group such as bread, pasta, and other grain-based foods. Fad diets don't work. People typically return to their old eating habits, and their weights go up. Following a fad diet long-term can lead to serious health problems later in life.

Slow and steady weight loss is the best way to go. Teens can lose weight by eating fewer calories. They can reach their target weight range more easily and quickly by eating less and increasing physical activity every day. If a weight-loss plan is not working, they can change it or develop a new plan. Learning and practicing healthy eating and exercise habits will lead to weight loss and life-long weight control.

Stress and Cholesterol

Over time, stress can raise blood cholesterol levels. The body reacts to stress by releasing cortisol and other brain chemicals. Cortisol stimulates the appetite, and some teens overeat, especially foods that are high in fat and sugar. The cholesterol and saturated fat in these foods can contribute to increased levels of total blood cholesterol. The excess food leads to weight gain. Responding to and coping with stress influences appetite and body composition.

Stress is a part of life. Positive stress is energizing and makes life fun and exciting. Negative stress directly affects physical and mental health. Sometimes teens can reduce stress. For instance, they might work less at part-time jobs to allow time for physical fitness.

Managing Stress

Developing and using stress management skills will help teens deal with stress. Managing stress means taking charge of emotions and thoughts and practicing healthy techniques. Physical activity like walking, biking, dancing, or playing sports is an effective way to handle stress. Deep breathing, muscle relaxation, stretching, yoga, and tai chi can clear the mind and relax the body. Teens might enjoy singing, daydreaming, or listening to relaxing music. Sometimes taking negative or pent-up energy and using it in useful ways helps a person regain a sense of calm. When feeling stressed,

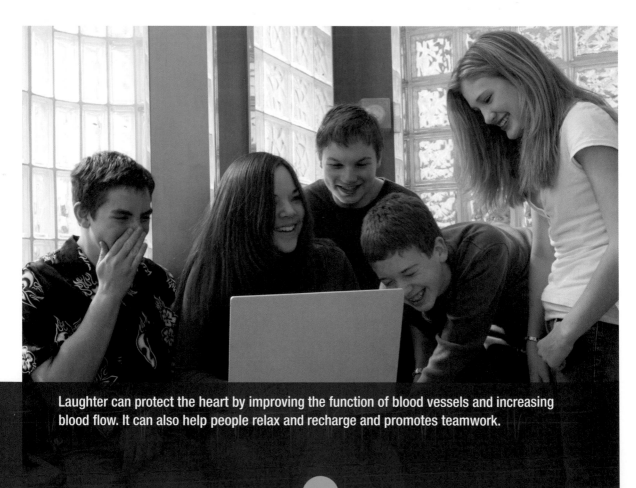

Laughter can protect the heart by improving the function of blood vessels and increasing blood flow. It can also help people relax and recharge and promotes teamwork.

teens might want to clean their bedroom, wash the car, or organize a collection. Some find that writing, drawing, or other creative pursuits like photography or playing a musical instrument can all help teens to unwind.

Laughing is a great way to deal with everyday stress. It provides good results right away. When laughing, more oxygen is taken in and moves through the bloodstream, which stimulates the circulatory system, lungs, and muscles. The brain makes more chemicals called endorphins (the body's natural pain relievers). After laughing, heart rate and blood pressure decrease, and people feel more relaxed. Laughter is also good long-term because it improves the immune system to help fight stress and illnesses.

Planning well leads to less stress. By planning, teens set and prioritize goals and budget their time. They schedule time for school, fitness, relaxation, sleep, and other important events. They also set deadlines and expectations that are realistic. Budgeting time helps them to balance school, work, exercise, time with friends and family, and time to help others.

By planning, teens can organize their day and reduce stress over what must get done. They will find it easier saying no so that they do not schedule too much to do. When overextended, many teens find it difficult to stay calm. Learn ways to manage stress through books, DVDs, or reputable Web sites. Teens can try different methods to determine what is effective for them.

Spending Time with Others

Positive, supportive, and encouraging people make managing stress easier. Teens can build a network of friends who help them cope in positive ways. Good friends are positive, enjoy humor, and make healthy choices. If possible, try to avoid people who use drugs, think negatively, or are often angry.

When going through a tough time, getting support can help teens deal with problems. They might want to confide in friends, a family member, or a counselor. They can join a support group for teens. These groups can be found in schools, clubs, and health facilities. Members of the support group exchange information and help each other develop healthy ways to cope with problems.

Teens might want to do something for someone else. This takes the focus away from their unhappy feelings and provides them with a fresh outlook. Many volunteer opportunities are available, such as helping causes like the environment or animals, or at a food bank or clothing donation center.

Getting Enough Sleep

Getting enough sleep is essential for good health. Most teens require nine or more hours of sleep every day. Not getting enough sleep can contribute to being overweight or obese. Teens who are overweight or obese tend to have higher levels of total blood cholesterol.

Sometimes poor sleep is due to medical problems that require a doctor's care. For example, poor sleep may be due to sleep apnea. People with this condition have difficulty breathing when asleep because they have shallow breathing or often stop breathing through-out the night. When they are not breathing, they wake up to start breathing again. The disorder causes increased amounts of stress hormones, including cortisol, to be released. As a result, teens who have sleep apnea may be overweight. Excess weight tends to increase

Some teens use television to fall asleep. However, television stimulates the mind because it is noisy. In addition, the continuous flickering light coming from the television can interfere with falling and staying asleep.

their blood pressures and heart rates, leading to a higher risk of developing cardiovascular disease and diabetes.

To get enough sleep, teens can make and stick to a regular sleep-wake schedule by planning their bedtime and sleep every day. Going to bed whenever schoolwork is done or after text messaging friends late at night does not work. To schedule sleep, teens may find that they need to adjust their bed-wake times. If so, they should take a week or two to make the changes. Teens should try to stick to their sleep schedule, even on weekends. Although the body can probably handle an occasional night of not enough sleep or poor-quality

What to Avoid or Limit to Improve Sleep

Teens may have habits that are keeping them awake at night. For example, consuming too much caffeine in the afternoon or evening can cause difficulty falling and staying asleep at night. It's a good idea to keep the daily limit of caffeine to the amount that is in two cups of regular coffee or two or three cans of caffeinated soda. Caffeine is also in energy drinks, teas, chocolate, coffee-flavored frozen desserts and gum, and some over-the-counter medicines. Heavy caffeine users might want to cut back gradually to avoid having headaches and feeling irritable and tired. Because the body digests food best when it is upright, eat two to three hours before bedtime and avoid fatty and spicy foods. Vigorous exercise close to bedtime prevents the body and mind from relaxing. Exciting or disturbing video or computer games, television, surfing the Internet, or communications with friends close to bedtime can also keep teens from falling asleep.

sleep, it's important to resume the usual sleep-wake schedule as soon as possible.

Following a calming bedtime routine helps a person let go of stress and relax the body. It takes about thirty minutes to prepare for sleep. Teens should turn off their computers, cell phones, iPods, and TVs. Then they can read, snuggle with a pet, or do another quiet activity that they will associate with bedtime. If feeling tense, they can try light stretching, deep breathing, or relaxation exercises. Background noise, such as having the television on, disrupts sleep. White noise, though, can be helpful. Some teens run a white noise machine or a fan during the night. Using earplugs helps block noise.

Tips for Better Sleep

Most people sleep best in cool temperatures. Teens may need to lower the temperature, open a window, or turn on a fan to cool down a hot bedroom. Light disrupts sleep, so teens should turn off lamps and overhead lights. Block all outside light, if possible.

At bedtime, most people tend to fall asleep within ten to twenty minutes. If they are still awake after twenty minutes, teens can get out of bed and do a quiet activity in their room. Return to bed when sleepy. Sometimes concerns keep people from falling asleep. One way to deal with this is to write the issues on paper. This can stop the mind from dwelling on problems and help teens fall asleep.

Taking a nap during the day can be refreshing. However, naps longer than twenty minutes can affect nighttime sleep. Naps are best in the late morning or early afternoon.

All these suggestions can result in acquiring healthy habits that can help lower cholesterol levels and maintain them. It takes practice and time to replace old lifestyle behaviors with new, healthier habits. Adopting positive habits now can help teens maintain good health in the years to come.

GLOSSARY

aerobic exercise Any physical activity that uses large muscle groups and increases the heart rate for a period of time.

atherosclerosis The buildup of waxy deposits (plaque) on the inside of blood vessels.

body mass index (BMI) A ratio of weight to height used to calculate body fat.

calorie A unit to measure energy or heat.

cardiovascular disease A medical disorder that affects the heart and blood vessels.

cholesterol A fatlike substance produced in the liver of all animals. It is found in foods of animal origin.

coordination The act of body parts working together smoothly and gracefully.

cross-training Combining two or more types of physical activity.

diabetes A disease that affects the way body cells convert food into energy.

flexibility The ability to move a body part through a full range of motion.

heart attack An interruption of the flow of blood to any part of the heart.

high-density lipoprotein (HDL) A type of cholesterol that picks up extra cholesterol out of cells and tissues and brings it to the liver. It helps protect against cardiovascular disease.

hormone A substance made by the body that circulates in the blood and has specific effects on the body.

hydrogenation The addition of hydrogen to vegetable oils to change them into solid fats.

lipoprotein A tiny package of proteins on the outside and fats inside that readily mix with blood to transport cholesterol to body tissues.

low-density lipoprotein (LDL) A type of cholesterol that carries more than half of the total blood cholesterol in the blood to tissues. Too much LDL in the blood can cause atherosclerosis.

obesity Excess body fat.

omega-3 fatty acid A type of "healthy fat" that can help reduce triglyceride levels and lower blood pressure. This fat is found in fatty cold-water fish like herring, tuna, salmon, trout, and mackerel.

plaque Fatty deposits that build up on the inside of artery walls. It is made up of cholesterol, fibrous tissue, calcium, and other cells.

posture The position of the body.

saturated fat A type of fat found naturally in red meat, poultry with skin, whole-milk foods, lard (pork fat), and tropical oils. This fat is usually solid or semisolid.

sleep apnea A condition in which a person stops breathing periodically during sleep.

stress The body and mind's reactions to demands or threats.

stroke An interruption of the flow of blood to any part of the brain.

trans fat A type of fat that is made by hydrogenation that changes oils to solids. This fat raises total and low-density lipoprotein and lowers high-density lipoprotein.

triglyceride A type of fat that provides much of the energy needed for cells to function.

unsaturated fat A type of fat found naturally in plant oils. This fat is usually liquid.

white noise Noise that produces a soothing sound that can mask more disturbing sounds.

American Diabetes Association
1701 North Beauregard Street
Alexandria, VA 22311
(800) 342-2383
Web site: http://www.diabetes.org
The American Diabetes Association funds research to prevent, cure,
and manage diabetes. It also provides information on healthy
eating and fitness.

American Heart Association
7272 Greenville Avenue
Dallas, TX 75231
(800) 242-8721
Web site: http://www.americanheart.org
The mission of the American Heart Association is to reduce deaths
resulting from cardiovascular disease and stroke.

American Medical Association
515 North State Street
Chicago, IL 60610
(800) 621-8335
Web site: http://www.ama-assn.org
The American Medical Association works to promote the art and
science of medicine and improving public health.

Centers for Disease Control and Prevention (CDC)
1600 Clifton Road

Atlanta, GA 30333

(800) CDC-INFO (232-4636)

Web site: http://www.cdc.gov

The CDC, a division of the U.S. Department of Health and Human
Services, is an excellent source of information on health
and fitness.

Health Canada

Brooke Claxton Building, Room 1264D

Tunney's Pasture

Postal Locator: 0912D

Ottawa, ON K1A 0K9

Canada

(866) 225-0709

Web site: http://www.hc-sc.gc.ca

Canada's federal agency helps people maintain and improve
their health.

National Cholesterol Education Program

NHLBI Health Information Network

P.O. Box 30105

Bethesda, MD 20824-0105

(301) 592-8573

Web site: www.nhlbi.nih.gov/about/ncep

The goal of the National Cholesterol Education Program is to
raise awareness and understanding about high blood
cholesterol.

National Heart, Lung, and Blood Institute
Building 31, Room 5A52
31 Center Drive MSC 2486
Bethesda, MD 20892
(301) 592 8573
Web site: http://www.nhlbi.nih.gov
The National Heart, Lung, and Blood Institute provides health information about the heart, lungs, and blood, including cholesterol,
healthy eating, physical fitness, and more.

National Institutes of Health (NIH)
9000 Rockville Pike
Bethesda, MD 20892
(301) 496-4000
Web site: http://www.nih.gov
The NIH is another division of the U.S. Department of Health and
Human Services. It conducts and supports medical research,
and like the CDC, is an excellent source of health information.

Office of Disease Prevention and Health Promotion (ODPHP)
National Health Information Center
P.O. Box 1133
Washington, DC 20013-1133
(800) 336-4797
Web site: http://odphp.osophs.dhhs.gov
The ODPHP has developed guidelines for physical activity for
Americans of all ages.

Public Health Agency of Canada
30 Colonnade Road
A.L. 6501H
Ottawa, ON K1A 0K9
Canada
(866) 225-0709
Web site: http://www.canadian-health-network.ca
The role of the Public Health Agency of Canada is to promote health
and prevent and control chronic diseases, such as cardiovascular
disease and diabetes.

Web Sites

Due to the changing nature of Internet links, Rosen Publishing has
developed an online list of Web sites related to the subject of this
book. This site is updated regularly. Please use this link to access
the list:

http://www.rosenlinks.com/hab/chol

Better Homes and Gardens. *Better Homes and Gardens Snack Attack!* Hoboken, NJ: Wiley, 2006.

Bijlefeld, Marjolijn, and Sharon K. Zoumbaris. *Food and You: A Guide to Healthy Habits for Teens*. Westport, CT: Greenwood, 2008.

Covey, Sean. *The 7 Habits of Highly Effective Teens Personal Workbook*. Forest City, NC: Fireside Books, 2003.

Espeland, Pamela, and Elizabeth Verdick. *Making Choices and Making Friends: The Social Competencies Assets*. Minneapolis, MN: Free Spirit Publishing, 2006.

Fletcher, Anne M. *Weight Loss Confidential Journal: Week-by-Week Success Strategies for Teens from Teens*. Boston, MA: Houghton Mifflin Harcourt, 2008.

Ford, Jean. *Right On Schedule!: A Teen's Guide to Growth and Development*. Philadelphia, PA: Mason Crest Publishers, 2005.

Fox, Annie. *Too Stressed to Think? A Teen Guide to Staying Sane When Life Makes You Crazy*. Minneapolis, MN: Free Spirit Publishing, 2005.

Goodger, Beverley. *Exercise*. North Mankato, MN: Smart Apple Media, 2006.

Hipp, Earl. *Fighting Invisible Tigers: A Stress Management Guide for Teens*. Minneapolis, MN: Free Spirit Publishing, 2008.

Hovius, Christopher. *The Best You Can Be: A Teen's Guide to Fitness and Nutrition*. Philadelphia, PA: Mason Crest Publishers, 2005.

Hyde, Margaret O., and Elizabeth H. Forsyth. *Stress 101: An Overview for Teens*. Minneapolis, MN: Twenty-First Century Books, 2007.

Moss, Samantha, and Lesley Schwartz. *Where's My Stuff? The Ultimate Teen Organizing Guide*. San Francisco, CA: Orange Avenue Publishing, 2007.

Naff, Clay Farris, ed. *Heart Disease*. Florence, KY: Gale Cengage Learning, 2008.

Purperhart, Helen, Barbara van Amelsfort, and Amina Marix Evans. *Yoga Exercises for Teens: Developing a Calmer Mind and a Stronger Body*. Alameda, CA: Hunter House, 2008.

Reber, Deborah. *Chill: Stress-Reducing Techniques for a More Balanced, Peaceful You*. New York, NY: Simon Pulse, 2008.

Rentz, Kristen. *YogaNap: Restorative Poses for Deep Relaxation*. Cambridge, MA: Da Capo Press, 2005.

Schroeder, Barbara, and Carrie Wiatt. *The Diet for Teenagers Only*. New York, NY: Harper Paperbacks, 2005.

Steinle, Jason. *Upload Experience: Quarterlife Solutions for Teens and Twentysomethings*. Evergreen, CO: Nasoj Publications, 2005.

Whittemore, Susan. *The Circulatory System*. Philadelphia, PA: Chelsea House, 2004.

Zinczenko, David. *Eat This Not That! for Kids!: Be the Leanest, Fittest Family on the Block!* Emmaus, PA: Rodale Books, 2008.

BIBLIOGRAPHY

American Academy of Pediatrics. "New AAP Policy on Lipid Screening and Heart Health in Children." July 7, 2008. Retrieved July 31, 2009 (http://www.aap.org/advocacy/releases/july08lipidscreening.htm).

American Heart Association. "Heart Disease and Stroke Statistics." 2009. Retrieved September 1, 2009 (http://www.americanheart.org/downloadable/heart/1240250946756LS-1982%20Heart%20 and%20Stroke%20Update.042009.pdf).

American Heart Association and American Stroke Association. "Understanding and Controlling Cholesterol." Booklet, 2007.

Brill, Janet. *Cholesterol Down: Ten Simple Steps to Lower Your Cholesterol in Four Weeks—Without Prescription Drugs*. New York, NY: Three Rivers Press, 2006.

Centers for Disease Control and Prevention. "Frequently Asked Questions (FAQs) About High Blood Cholesterol." April 9, 2009. Retrieved July 27, 2009 (http://www.cdc.gov/cholesterol/faqs.htm).

Centers for Disease Control and Prevention. "Healthy Weight—It's Not a Diet, It's a Lifestyle!" May 19, 2009. Retrieved July 27, 2009 (http://www.cdc.gov/healthyweight/children/index.html).

Centers for Disease Control and Prevention. "Leading Causes of Death." July 24, 2009. Retrieved July 27, 2009 (http://www.cdc.gov/nchs/FASTATS/lcod.htm).

Centers for Disease Control and Prevention. "Overweight and Obesity." May 15, 2009. Retrieved July 26, 2009 (http://www.cdc.gov//obesity/childhood/prevalence.html).

Centers for Disease Control and Disease Prevention. "Prevalence of Abnormal Lipid Levels Among Youths–United States, 1999– 2006." *Morbidity and Mortality Weekly Report*, Volume 59,

Number 2, January 22, 2010. Retrieved January 22, 2010 (http://www.cdc.gov/mmwr/PDF/wk/mm5902.pdf).

DeVane, Matthew S. *Heart Smart: A Cardiologist's 5-Step Plan for Detecting, Preventing, and Even Reversing Heart Disease*. Hoboken, NJ: Wiley, 2006.

Freeman, Mason, and Christine Junge. *The Harvard Medical School Guide to Lowering Your Cholesterol*. New York, NY: McGraw-Hill, 2005.

Lipsky, Martin, and Marla Mendelson, Stephan Havas, and Michael Miller. *American Medical Association Guide to Preventing and Treating Heart Disease*. Hoboken, NJ: Wiley, 2008.

Lopez, Ralph I. *The Teen Health Book: A Parent's Guide to Adolescent Health and Well-Being*. New York, NY: W. W. Norton, 2003.

National Heart, Lung, and Blood Institute. "Your Guide to Lowering Your Cholesterol with TLC: Therapeutic Lifestyle Changes." December 2005. Retrieved September 4, 2009 (http://www.nhlbi.nih.gov/health/public/heart/chol/chol_tlc.pdf).

National Stroke Association. "Cholesterol and Stroke." 2009. Retrieved July 28, 2009 (http://www.stroke.org/cholestcrol).

National Women's Health Resource Center. "Lower Your Cholesterol with Heart Healthy Choices." 2009. Retrieved September 1, 2009 (http://www.healthywomen.org/wellness/dietnutrition/loweryourcholesterolwithhearthealthychoices).

Rinzler, Carol Ann, and Martin W. Graf. *Controlling Cholesterol for Dummies*. Hoboken, NJ: Wiley, 2008.

U.S. Department of Health and Human Services. "2008 Physical Activity Guidelines for Americans." 2008. Retrieved September 1, 2009 (http://www.health.gov/paguidelines).

INDEX

A

aerobic fitness, 34–35, 37, 39, 40
American Academy of Pediatrics (AAP),
    14, 34
American Heart Association, 14, 17, 26
atherosclerosis, 9, 10, 12

B

balance training, 34, 36–37, 39
body mass index (BMI), 42–43

C

caffeine, 50
cancer, 6
cardiovascular disease, 5–6, 7, 9, 10, 11,
    12, 13, 17, 31, 49
Centers for Disease Control and
    Prevention (CDC), 6, 43
cholesterol,
    controlling, 7–17
    definition of, 4–6, 10
    diet and, 4, 6, 7, 13, 17, 18–29, 30, 42
    exercise and, 6, 13, 17, 29, 31–39
    main types of, 10–11
    myths and facts about, 30
    stress and, 13, 28, 32, 35, 45–47
    weight and, 4–5, 6, 13, 14, 33, 40, 41,
        42–45, 48–49
cholesterol levels, testing, 14,
    16–17, 41
core exercise, 34, 35–36, 39
cortisol, 45, 48
cross-training, 38–39

D

deep breathing, 32, 46, 50
diabetes, 6, 12, 13, 14, 33, 49

D (continued)

Dietary Guidelines for Americans, 22, 24, 29
dieticians, 26, 29, 43

E

eggs, 4, 7, 18, 22, 30
endorphins, 47
endurance activity, 34

F

fad diets, 44–45
fiber, 24, 25, 29, 41
fitness centers, 37–38, 40
fitness plan, sticking with a, 38–40
food diary, keeping a, 28
food labels, reading, 28

G

goals, setting, 38, 43

H

health professional, ten great questions
    to ask a, 41
heart attack, 6, 7, 9, 10, 12, 17, 31
heart disease, 7, 12, 14, 17
high blood pressure, 6, 13, 14, 49
high cholesterol,
    medicines for, 4, 14, 41
    risk factors for, 6, 11–13, 14, 17
    symptoms of, 17
high-density lipoprotein (HDL), 10, 12,
    14, 30, 31, 42
hydrogenation, 21

L

linoleic acid, 18
lipid panel/profile, 14

About the Author

Judy Monroe Peterson has earned two master's degrees, including a master's in public health education, and is the author of more than fifty educational books for young people. She is a former health care, technical, and academic librarian and college faculty member; biologist and research scientist; and curriculum writer and editor with more than twenty-five years of experience. She has taught courses at 3M, the University of Minnesota, and Lake Superior College. Currently, she is a writer and editor of K–12 and post–high school curriculum materials on a variety of subjects, including health, life skills, biology, life science, and the environment.

Photo Credits